To float, to drown,
to close up, to open

E. ALEX PIERCE

*To float, to drown,
to close up, to open*

UNIVERSITY *of* ALBERTA PRESS

Published by
University of Alberta Press
1-16 Rutherford Library South
11204 89 Avenue NW
Edmonton, Alberta, Canada   T6G 2J4
uap.ualberta.ca

**Library and Archives Canada
Cataloguing in Publication**
Title: To float, to drown, to close up, to open /
    E. Alex Pierce.
Names: Pierce, E. Alex, 1943– author.
Series: Robert Kroetsch series.
Description: Series statement:
    Robert Kroetsch series | Poems.
Identifiers: Canadiana (print) 20190069961 |
    Canadiana (ebook) 20190069945 |
    ISBN 9781772124538 (softcover) |
    ISBN 9781772124613 (PDF)
Classification: LCC PS8631.I469 T64 2019 |
    DDC C811/.6—dc23

First edition, first printing, 2020.
First printed and bound in Canada by
Houghton Boston Printers, Saskatoon,
Saskatchewan.
Copyediting by Peter Midgley.

A volume in the Robert Kroetsch Series.

University of Alberta Press is committed to protecting our natural environment. As part of our efforts, this book is printed on Enviro Paper: it contains 100% post-consumer recycled fibres and is acid- and chlorine-free.

University of Alberta Press gratefully acknowledges the support received for its publishing program from the Government of Canada, the Canada Council for the Arts, and the Government of Alberta through the Alberta Media Fund.

Canadä Canada Council   Conseil des Arts
for the Arts   du Canada   Alberta
                                  Government

For the grandmothers

Annie Maude Crouse Pierce
Mary Mitchell Swansburg Lloyd

and
Jennie Anderson Pierce

CONTENTS

Coda, Aubade.

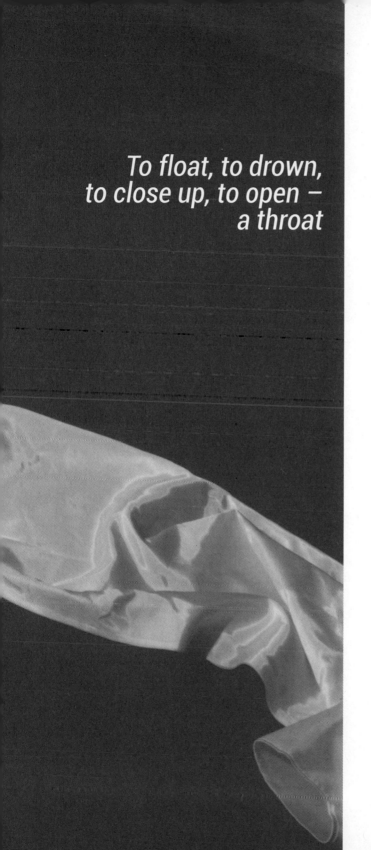

To float, to drown,
to close up, to open –
a throat

To float, to drown, to close up, to open – a throat

where the great artery rises and crosses, coming so close
to the larynx, the lynx in larynx, the animal voice
in its first low growl –

Over the kitchen table, night, after lamp is lit, voices
of the grandmother and grandfather lifting into the low beams
of the small old house, the pitch rough.

Under the low roof in the attic above we can hear them
after we stop giggling. Together we shut out
the fear of the dark. The black so black,
nights with no moon. The beds so deep we drift
down to sleep. Into feathers and flannel –

their sounds lifting and falling,
a mixture of stove black and coal tar,
hardwood and well water, its taste startling
cold, up out of the ground. The sounds
coming into us – into me. The green painted table,
curved chair backs, the brown teapot, cracked and porous –
still there – grandfather's axe, biting
into the root of the apple tree blown over by wind: *There's life in it yet.*
Haul it back up. The oxen, the ropes, the straining – August apples,
Yellow Transparents – the best ones, worth saving.

The things that enter you before you know
you're breathing in – the things that grab hold of the voice box,
climb up into the throat. Sound of the pig squeal
muffled, shut out, morning of the pig death, the cauldron
prepared, great vat of scalding water, the kids all sent down the hill
to play by the shore. The scream, the blood – was there a shot?
Heard or imagined, which is worse –

The sound of crab apples running down the chute to the pig's trough –
only yesterday – and milk, a bucket of milk and slop for the hungry,
vociferous sow – clean sided, white and pink, bright eyed,
sweet. Down by the river shore, the dragonfly with its darning needle –
It will come and sew up your mouth – lighting on the river rocks,
landing on some kid's arm. The river water soft – half fresh,
half salt. It tastes so good in your mouth. Cadence coming with the tide,
turning tongue of the tidal river lifting the small soft fragments of rock,
each piece worn, flat – from shale, from sandstone, from slate,
enough mica from granite to make it sparkle – tiny pieces
stuck to the soles of your feet. Lap of the arriving water,
pressing into the shore, the river's edge graduated, sheltered –
its language erasing now, the sounds civilized, modulated.
Sound of the lawn mower – old sharp scrape of the whetstone
waiting in its can of rusty water to edge and hone the scythe.

Language tied to the land – translated, embedded,
repeated, remembered, half lost. The crab apples
all run over the ground. Worms in them, sow bugs
in the fence posts, thousands of shingle flies.

The slain pig, white carcass stretched from a rafter
in the dim, forbidden barn.

To float, to drown, to open, to close up – a heart:
arch of the aorta, rounded over the valentine, its upper border
an inch below the top of the breast bone –

                              In the woodshed –
a girl picks up the sharpened hatchet, selects the best piece of pine,
(no knots) places it on the block. One, two – she is making a boat,
pointed bow, straight stern. Her grandfather will growl if he sees her
in here – but he knows. All the kids do it – she works in secret.
Pieces fit together, a cabin, a bridge. Shingle nails line the deck
to make a railing outlined with string. She cannot get
enough string. The boat is beautiful. After dinner she takes it
to the river shore. This is the summer of Uncle Jack – the girl is eleven.

When she is eighteen, she visits him – and Aunt Peggy, most beautiful
of the aunts – in Montreal. She goes to a concert in a slender dress, he
buys her a gardenia, a record – Dinu Lipatti playing Mozart. He says
he wants to be a writer, that the old people in Sable River are important
that they have changed his life. She wants to fall to her knees when she sees him.
She wants to press her forehead into the door frame and breathe him in.

The summer she is eleven, he takes her to Johnson's Pond,
pitches golf balls into the sand. She follows him down the beach —
he flashes his smile at her. She runs away when she sees him
drinking beer with the other uncles at the open trunk of the car.

All that is left is a photograph: Jack in his air force uniform — light
grey wool, hair slicked back. The smile. *He drank* —

Heart squeezed — barbed wire on the top strand of the fence,
cows in the pasture, alder switch flicking their sides to make them run.
Full river, dark brown water from the Tom Tigney flowing down to
meet the Sable's tide. Swimming holes. Kids swinging on the rope,
upriver, tied to the maple tree. Uncle Jack with his camera. Seeing
from the outside — making her beautiful. Jack
on the swinging bridge, kissing someone else —

To close up, to open – the piano, heart soaring. You can feel
a pulse beating there, just where the clavicle
articulates with the sternum, that same little hollow. Smell
of the practice rooms. Wood and varnish. Felts on the hammers.
Precision. Bach, Scarlatti. Running scales. Heart breaking –
every piano lesson a mission. Breath in the line, perfect
rendition. Never – never, never. A sonata by Scarlatti: sent to Portugal
to compose for the Princesa Maria Bárbara, he finds his form. Two pages,
diptych. Mirror. Listen – reverse symmetry. Here, the theme modulated
tonic to dominant: page two, dominant back to tonic. A closed world –
she can live there. Love knots form harmonic clusters, melodic line driven
into the page. Shoulders retract over the keyboard. A prelude
by Bach unbends the line. Care, care, in every chromatic interval.
Glenn Gould will take the whole tissue, render it perfect. Until then,
her girl's heart believes the mission. She will strike each note into the listener's
yearning heart – will play in the basement room of the little house on
Zwicker Ave, in Liverpool, for her mother's closest friends. Music, music –
live – in the room. The damp air, the red and blue tile floor, the
Heintzman upright. One day, one day – she will take the stage,
drown in the Steinway grand, its gold interior. Burn, inside out –
for the sound, transformation of sound.

Two houses, one up the road, one down – sand hills in between. River run
salt, at low tide an arm of the sea. Clam flats stretching along the channel –
the Sable River, stopped up by sadness on a perfect June day. Cortège
of cars at the tiny cemetery, mid-way.

The smaller house, whitewashed, old – facing the river – green trim.
We can see it from the rowboat. Sides banked with eelgrass for winter,
windows caulked. Rags of grass and wind. Low roof, ell chamber –

At twelve, and in sorrow unable to speak, outside
the spare white church – waiting for the line of cars
to pass.
                   Up at the small house, kids running loose
in the yard – cousins, three to a bed. Grandfather
out by the sawed-off August-apple tree. Codfish
hanging up to dry. Everything bitter, salt, vital,
quick. Wood stove roaring hot. A smell of creosote
and tar. Rich taste of beans baked with salt pork and molasses.
Sound of iron on iron – the dinner gong. Oil lamp
on the kitchen table. Kerosene light on the grandmother's face.
White hair, yellowed, pulled up in a knot. Voices
growling – rising and falling, out
into the seamless dark.

The other house, the one down the road – the other
grandparents – big house with its spruce timber frame,
oak staircase, maple hardwood, polished floors. Smell
of lemon oil rubbed into the dining-room table. Walls
the colour of verdigris, painted border. Scroll work in the ceilings,
swirl of the plasterer's hawk.

                                 Mitred corners in the crown moulding
at the top of the parlour walls. The diamond window in the entryway –
patches of amber, of ochre, carnelian red and acid green,
rose madder and cobalt blue – glass to filter light, run riot on
the warm hardwood floor, names learned from the twisted tubes
of oil paint in the little room upstairs where grandmother
mixed her colours for the canvasses stretched on the pegged
hand-made frames. Legs and arms of the children patterned
in coloured light.

Pump organ in the parlour corner, voices deep and slow,
his more a rumble than a snore – hers, a schoolteacher's voice,
'Now then, now then.' *Guide me, O Thou great Jehovah* – pumping
the pedals to the floor, filling the bellows, making the cracked
lungs sing. Grampie's Welsh bass opening up – *Bread of heaven,*
Bread of heaven, Feed me 'til I want no more... Faux bourdon, Flute, Oboe,
Celeste: organ-stops lettered in Gothic script. *Vox humana*, the human voice,
slight tremolo in the organ's reeds: *Vox angelica* – higher pitched,
greater trembling, unbearably sweet. The middle voices doubling,
joining all, an orchestra of sound in the corniced parlour. The stiff sofa,
its swooped back, Pot of Gold, Moirs chocolates hidden underneath,
the little map, its outline clear to locate every treasure – praline,
nougat, candied ginger, coffee crème – *enrobé de chocolat*. Above
the sofa, castles on the Rhine, moonlight, ships at anchor –
one of her paintings in a gold leaf frame.

Open on the music stand beside the hymnal, Stephen Foster:
Camptown ladies sing this song — Doo-dah, doo-dah —
Camptown Racetrack five miles long — Oh, de doo-dah day —

In the kitchen, a dozen lemons squeezed into the pale green
Depression-glass measuring cup to make lemon meringue pie
for Sunday, when the minister would come to dinner.
Twelve o'clock sharp, after church.
                                        Grandmother Lloyd's
purse snapping shut after she dispensed peppermints
and change for the collection plate — the wooden plates
felt-lined so the money wouldn't clink — & folded envelopes
full of weekly pledges, printed in red and black ink.

Smell of the pigeon-holed desk in the hallway of the house — glue,
paper, the potpourri — dried rose petals, cinnamon & cloves.
Gummed labels, tags for keys, iron boat full of copper pennies,
blue overseas envelopes —

Canvas mailbag waiting to hang outside
on the post. Easter lilies in boxes sent from Bermuda, drugging us
with their heavy, anointed smell. Half of them for the church,
where their scent floated into the new varnish, penetrated the wood
and made us wheeze and dream. *Praise him, praise him, all ye*
little children. Praise *her* — whispered to my secret self.

The rising snores at naptime — chamber pots
in all the bedrooms, butter yellow sun lancing the beds.
Dream time. One hundred yellow *National Geographics*
with pictures of pygmies and crocodiles, naked Black women,
startling to see, lips extended by scallop shells, and necks
encased in rings. Mission box
on the upstairs hall table —
                            Some afternoons the house smelled
of turpentine and linseed oil. When did she paint — we never saw her.
Sometimes the door ajar, the wooden paint box left open,
the easel, covered. She must have stood there, working
in the last, late afternoon light — grandmother poised over
a hawk's wing, detail of a clawed foot stuck in the
partridge's opened bloody breast. 'Why would you
hang that in your dining room,' my father asks.
'Because she painted it.'

                    Studies of tulips, of
light refracted on glass, and pressed dried grasses, ferns,
common weeds – she knew all their Latin names:

Spiraea latifolia, Tanacetum vulgare, Linaria vulgaris –
meadowsweet, common tansy, butter-and-eggs – the roadsides
lined with lupines, gardens full of sweet pea, tiger lily,
purple columbine. Creamy honeysuckle climbing
all over the porch railing – the *verandah*. Bees intoxicated
on clover – we sucked the nectar from the pink and white
tips: *Trifolium pratense* (three leaflets, of meadows),
monarch butterfly, luna moth – everything
with a classification and a name. Bleeding heart,
Dicentra. Digitalis, foxglove. Slide your finger
into its spotted throat – tiny hairs to guide the bee. Grampie,
in the bedroom, drinking nitre from a silver christening cup.

'His heart is weak. Be still and let him rest.' Not a word from us.
Even the wind stopped. Glare of the afternoon light
over all the objects. Dust of the afternoon light in all the spaces,
blinds half pulled. Weight of waiting. Flies still on the windowpane.

A chorus from the church, cracked voices stretching up
into the varnished ceiling. To float, I almost drowned –

Girl, too tall, in a printed pink cotton dress, puffed sleeves,
wanting to run. Stiff backs of the men, grey gloves,
carrying the closed coffin away from the hearse –

Vair me oh-ro van-o, Vair me oh-ro van-e – played
on the pipes. Did it save me – strap of the aorta,
little hanger, the strap by which we hold to life –

September, far away from home, off Ingonish Beach,
the ocean's swell seductive – pulling me in, dragging me
back out, fingers torn, crawling up onto the rocks.
Yellow bladders of the seaweed splitting open. Echoing
above the rocks, song of the old grandmothers –

Vair me oh-ro, oh-ho –
Sad am I, without thee.

Hours in the practice rooms. Forty-eight preludes and fugues,
Bach's *Well-Tempered Clavier*. Note spoken unto note: nothing
will separate her from her audience. How can that be –
to think into the music, send out the sound, have the sound
received. She practices late at night in the cold of a church vestry,
bends the rules, forces the notes on a hard, old piano,
leaves the safety of the conservatory. Fingers
swell. She fails her third-year exam. Music
abandons her, no one sees
and no one hears.

        Imagine a heart willing – anything –
to speak. Imagine the aorta in its slow rise toward the throat. Curve
of the great artery descending now from its brave arch, reaching backward
and down over the root of the left lung. Imagine the bronchi, their soft,
spongy alveoli – florets receiving blood-borne air.

The startled faces of her teachers when she stops
mid-fugue. A look, almost satisfaction, then –
compassion – on the face of the one she'd left. Changed
for the demanding austerity of the elusive, elegant
tall grey man. Head of the conservatory, he speaks in images,
breaks open her bright determination.

Two grand pianos in a darkened room. His singing tone
accompanying hers, weight on the keys, loss of airy Mozart.
Even the dark fantasias –

She has fought hard in the arena, plunged into the Beethoven
he assigns her. One of the diabolical sonatas, all pattern and bravura. Technique,
and skill. No passion no tenderness.
At least, not for her.

She hides – practices now in the organ loft above the chapel,
whispering, singing, following the chromatic intervals of the Bach prelude,
A-minor, close to the blood, modal, plaintive –

The way hands touch an instrument, caress, struggle,
flow, become water – pulling toward this confluence of the eye,
heart, mind.

Bach, in the dark, the melodic lines converging. Counterpoint.
Lines of sound – they fit one another.

The little organ, soft to the touch. Ease
for the injured hands. Prayer, really.
She is broken. Her desire to tell the world something,
everything, all collapsed inward.

So much she wanted to bring – to a listening world.

It does not matter now. It does. She is walking through snow.
The mind testing, pressing, speaking. Search – in A-minor.
Sheep may safely graze... Sheep would die
in this storm. Folding. In. They must
come into the fold.

She surrenders. She sees the sheep lying down,
she works out the fingering, slides her thumb
under the knuckles, the flat of her hand. As Bach instructed.

Such a small thing, the gliding thumb.
After such a great fall.

In her final year she
makes her way to the piano again. Beethoven stands in the corner of a room –
Beethoven, with his cracked heart, his broken plates, his piss pots,
piles of garbage, cold blank windows – his sublime indifference to all
that is not music. Beethoven with his shuttered ear, his majestic interior,
his ruined performances, his bleak, cold, sinewy days.

It is clear how she loves him. The introduction, spoken
to the audience, is an apology for love. *This is Beethoven's*
tender period, the interlude before the deafness settles in –

The great 110, in A-flat major. In the conservatory, the narrow rooms,
wood echoing sound. How does a heart creep into the wood that lines
the walls. How does sweat seep into the windowsills, the casings.
How does the pressure of this man's need translate her longing into
elegant sound.
                    It is the hand holding the heart. The hand that, skilled,
disciplined, articulating the written notes, carries the pulsing fist-sized
pump that beats out measured time. This moment, this moment –

She will live with him, with the great sonatas, give him every breath
of her sweet, quick, intelligence – her skill, her youth. She will breathe
into his line, lift into the arc of his phrasing, unlock the impenetrable rooms.

Her mother books passage on a Cunard liner. The girl resists, summer arrives.
Her shadowy muse gives way. Perhaps it was Beethoven who accompanied her –
He who carried her across. Perhaps she does not carry, as she thought, his flame.

To float, to drown, to enter, close up – a house.
Her father tears the small house down – sets fire
to the wreckage while she and her mother, in England,
enter Shakespeare's wooden O. Hearts pounding – the aorta, now,
plunging straight down, pierces the diaphragm's barrier. Blood travels
from lungs to vitals, nothing remains untouched. A tiny replica of Shakespeare's
Globe waits for her in England's Stratford-upon-Avon. The histories
in all their gaudy seriousness play upon the Stratford stage. The
little O, the story rooms, the childlike road, the boy Will's journey
into London. Throne room, costumes. Exhibitions capture
all her fancy, throw her back, and forward, take her head
and turn it round. Fourth row, centre – a fire burns, but in her
mind: *Henry V*, the Chorus – a single actor in Elizabethan doublet,
a single voice – light in the breathing dark.

There is nothing in the space – and everything is there. More
than music, more than want. The aorta splits, half to the right side,
half to the left   curves past the iliac crests. In the flames, her father
and her brother wet gunny sacks and throw them over grandmother's lilac
bushes. Smoke gushes out from the tarred beams. *Now all the youth
of England* – her father, in a white shirt, standing over the timbers.
Blood finds its channel into the spleen. Prince Hal is Henry now,
old alliances fall away. He remakes his world –

Timber and sash, plaster board and painted ceiling, shingle
and frame (her mother's hand on the paintbrush,
making the old house new). Gone, gone –

gone. And here, in the breathing space,
a light, a voice – an invitation... *behold the threaden sails,
Borne with th'invisible and creeping wind...*

And everything that burns must burn. Her father pours gasoline,
her brother beside him in the flames. Eelgrass, for insulation
to bank the house in winter. Mouse nest, squirrel rummage,
rat pile and linings of newspaper. Oilcloth, linoleum, fir plank
and cheap fibre wallboard — all the attempts
at meagre renovation —
                              door frames, window casings: he saves
the family Bible, the lists of all their names. What does he do with his
mother's things? His father's? Their clothes, her dresser, the contents
of her pantry — the little narrow room from which emerged the pans
of rolls and biscuits, the rising loaves of bread ready for baking
in the hot wood-stove oven. What does he do with her stove?

Hear the shrill whistle —
                              The wild boy is king now — and everything
is changed. The great artery, in two parts, lets blood downward
into the legs. Action, action! (Her mother knows, but doesn't speak.)
The play, the play — the English cross the channel, into France.

And in that space of summer afternoon, the image born of sound
and light inhabits all her blood and bone, the mind ignites. She sees
the fire — space for her is stage now, theatre is the flame. She sees it
burning all the way back to the Sable River, the lamp, the voices,
the two old people, in the dark,
without wall or roof or post
or beam —
                and even as her father buries refuse
in the cellar hole, turns all this under, she
seizes it, picks up her torch,
and runs.

Full Moon

When it's full moon on the Sable River bar, high tide is always eight o'clock —
her father gives her this, from Everett, his father. He gives her
the dog whistle, a canvas bucket, a new lawn mower, his breaking heart.
Nor' nor' east, nor' east, east nor' east — east. Boxing the compass.
East sou' east, sou' east — he stands in the kitchen of the new house
he built so long ago. He can't do the yard work anymore.
Can't pile in the hardwood they need for winter.
His old language coming back — *Wood for winter, hoe potatoes,*
haul the eelgrass, brace the sled.

She drives his truck and runs it off the icy road. Rolls it. *This was my life,*
he says — *my life.* A bucket full of sorrow. Pays someone to haul the truck
away, repair it, keep it. Over. The way they tell their stories. Plain.
Heroes in this place of river tide and ocean storm, of deer kill and
wild-goose, wildcat and porcupine. His Christmas tree lot,
the poison used to kill the maples killing him. His measure
over every acre of his land — lengths still counted out
in chains. His steady cadence, how that falls
and wraps her. No more sorrow, no.

Twig and fire and breath of wind —
window's rattle. The end of him.

The Sable River empties into the bay, running westward onto Louis Head.
It splits its channel either side of John's Island, touches the Ferry Lane
on the east – our side – then mingles with the salt sea water,
reaching almost to the creek. The sand bars make a backbone
up the bay, and seals come in to lie there. Once
I found a seal pup on the shore, alive and hissing.

Before there was the bridge, upriver, people used to holler to the ferryman
to row the dory over and take them back and forth. And now
the bridge is gone, the pilings left, our Ferry Lane a small path
through the woods that runs down to a sheltered beach.

And who can find the path our mothers took us to –
and named it. (We thought it meant the *fairy* lane.)

My father knew the names of every one in every house, West side,
East side – up and down the Sable River. Foss Lisk's place, opposite
his house, across the river where Blanche would watch, and phone up
when she saw their car come in the yard. *I've been looking for your light.*

A signal, when night was black and full moon an event
that every creature waited for. To hunt, or hide, or plot,
or seize, or court. Full moon late in August. Cut the alders,
take a run down to the beach to see the moon come straight up
from the water. Like the first time, the only time. Breakers
rolling in, the ancient sound of breath – on rock.

I will cherish the old rugged cross
Till my trophies at last I lay down —

He lies in the bed, their bed, in the last bedroom.
And he is alone. His face when we tell him,
She's gone. There are things not to write.

If you've been there you'll know.

The others are in the kitchen: my brother, the women,
my sister and her husband gone home. I continue to sing
after the big hymns are finished. Anything that comes to me.

He is here and not here. *An old lion*, he said.
I do not want to say how he looks. There is little of him left —
and he wants so badly to stay.

Laughter. They are tired. Her, last week, the funeral —
him now. He pushes against the pale blue navy-trimmed pyjamas.
His chest pushes out as he makes the effort to breathe.

They need you, Dad. They need you on the other side.
He looks at me. *They do?*
The tide is going.

He gets into the boat. He gets into the boat and pushes off —
a channel opens up past the sandflats, and the dark brown river water slides
over the deep clear salt water

out toward the sea.

He sits up straight and straighter, his familiar back, his arms, pull the oars.

And I am no longer in the stern of the boat
where I can see his face.

The boy. The boy is her beloved.

I visited them in Martin's River at the brick house Uncle Don Langille built,
my Aunt Connie and Brian, her son born nearly sixty years ago, with Down's.

He lives with her now, comes to the kitchen and hugs me once he is sure of the voice,
its tenor. He may be waiting for me to calm down. She is ninety, gives me tea, the last

of my father's sisters and brothers, the last of that line. A phone call from the car, knock
on the door, and she lets me in. Her voice with a little catch, a high note, hasn't changed.

A kind of caressing, a laugh in it. She's the youngest, blond (was), closest to my father,
the youngest son. Brian stopped growing, stayed alive. 'He's the one who never

left me,' she says, just before I go. I pull out of the driveway where we stopped
every time we drove from Liverpool to Halifax, on the old Number 3.

For the first time in all the years, I go left and drive to the end of the Martin's River Road, then
turn back. And I see them. They don't see me. They're standing

side by side. Aunt Connie and her little son, my cousin. Waiting for the car to go by.
Out for their walk. In the afternoon light.

Not little. Her son. Radiant
afternoon light.

Medway River, Carousel

The carousel cresting down the Medway River, half submerged, the horses dragging. It's floating
now, the horses turning on the water. We used to drive past it at the fairgrounds in Caledonia,

boarded up in a green painted building. I'm standing here staring into the water – in the dark
shoulder of this late November night. I'm eight, or is it twelve, running when the momentum

slows just enough to allow us on – and I'm afraid. Upriver is a small house and inside is a sick girl
counting hours and pills, holding on. I phone, she's slow to answer. Don't come. Not tonight.

We're running for the carousel, I don't wait for my little sister, making sure I get a horse, not
a stupid turkey or donkey, even a rooster. What's the point! I grab on and hold the reins, stare

into the oiled brass fittings turning up and down, the pull, the feel of flying. I lean out
and look for our parents in the crowd, as close as I'll ever get to riding – a real horse. I'm

seeing the whole curving thing now careening down the Medway – standing here
beside my car, the water close to flooding. There's my thirteen-year-old self, too tall

for the horses, still wanting to ride, wanting with all that awful want that never fills, leaning
out in the saddle, pretending, except it's all too real. The crowd, the painted boards, the horses

here only these few days, the raucous music, smell of pink spun cotton and the juicy rush
of a McIntosh apple, bitten through the bright red candy covering that almost cracks

your teeth. Dad in a shirt and tie, talking with a salesman he knows – it's as if I've never
seen him before. The crowded exhibition hall, room after room of drawings up on

the walls, pictures from every grade-school in Queen's County, even ours. Walking
until you could fall down, boys on the steps, smoking, not one of them sees me, I'm glad

they don't. Fairground dirt, the animal barns low and quiet, the cattle steaming
in their stalls, ribbons, kids. It's night and I'm folded, years later, into Teddy's car,

streaming out to Black Point, Queensland, there's a carousel he wants to photograph, two
horses, small magic thing, icon from his pictures. I'm wearing the satin zip-up jacket

that says *Immaculata*, high-school beauty queen, a silver mask, thirty-eight going on
seventeen. We make the shot, the wind's wet and we curl back in the car, already

almost out of love, still playing artist and model, for keeps, animating every perfect still
he ever made, peopling all the blank, dark frames, making lipstick marks on the platinum

pages of his former lives. I'm the mistress
of impossible things. Upriver, the sick girl reaches for her water glass,

the blue containers. Her lists. She's ready,
grabs a mane.
                              And now the river takes it all, carries
our adolescent wishes between the rocks, along
the swirl and wash and flow

and drive and beat. The carousel, it's coming toward us,
lifting us onto the platform with the painted horses,
water-sloshed and broken, cresting

their coarse and tangled manes, hind legs
reared up, forelegs pawing – the thing
can't last, it's going down, down

the river, the horses sliding, swimming – nothing's
drowning but our dreams. Water black,
then silver, coiling,

slipping, buckling – cherry-stained
and iron-red
beneath.

Nothing more lonely

                  than those tail lights
turning the corner, red against the snow,
my mother inside, her last ride from home.

I stood there, for the measured silence,
drove in my car to my cousin's house
awake all night from the shock, the shift —

Less than, more than, impossible to
compare, the roof torn off the house
something no longer there.

The Creek

When the light changes, day-shadow crawls across the lawn, black
suddenly. Arrived from slow increment, the day the eye's mind registers
the end of summer. Black-green between the blades of grass,
black-green in the spaces between the apple leaves, the green still green
but dark in every place a shadow finds to form. In folds of cloth, a dress
hung on the clothesline, its looping skirt a shape,
a missing body — someone gone.

All the opened spaces filling up, containers holding light.
Thick, liquid, ochre and umber — rich, august,
inexorable — a hand upon your arm. Come. Now.

To float, to drown — to open, close up —

To attend, watch, alliterate, mourn with the outflow —
that words might come, consequence of creek's, of river's
mouth — spilling constant, river-borne and tidal, pulling in
and flowing out. To follow down through field to pasture,
marsh, the land below the other house.

To arrive at, to attain — the creek:
a long channel, and a lung, for drawing in
for flinging out, the golden water, moving, steady —
dark-trembled in a braid — from the peat water
washing down, black-brown, iron-red, running,
coursing all its minerals into the water-brook, the brook
that makes the creek. Rhodora at its edges in the spring,
sheep's laurel, alder, ash, and hackmatack, wild
pear, and wild cherry —

              And I, its given – shadow,
accompaniment, like cloud's mark on land on a high
summer's day, the meaning of footfall – to run here
from childhood to now. Not chosen,
only seen, caught up, spit out –

The water draining down – from sphagnum moss and golden-root,
black spruce and bake apple, cranberry, alder catkin, lady's slipper
(guarded, hidden), huckleberry, choke cherry, bunchberry
filling the cut tracks of the sled road, sea grass and lamb's quarters,
goose tongue greens and sea lavender, wild barley, a patch of bitter lovage,
and marsh grass – so sharp it cuts your feet.

The brook water sluiced clean across the granite stones –
remnants of a crossing place – pulled across the marshland,
gurgling out of its opening throat, disgorged into the sea
where the waves turn brown to meet it,
sharp sea water turning gold to meet it
coming back.

              And I, its child,
barely human, its spare, salt, wild thing sent to run
along its edges, float along its edges – only like shorebird,
Sandpiper and Willet, to tip, plane along the sand that breaks
and falls, dissolves and makes new edge at every tide –

This is what will happen when I die –

My mouth will become the creek's mouth, and my throat
will slide into its channel. My lungs will spread out over the saltmarsh.

Water from the water-brook will pour out and make its gurgling sound.

I will lie face down.
My windpipe will become the passageway —

My gut will lower itself into the swimming hole, the wings of the iliac crest
scoop out a basin.

My pubic bone will find its way into the sand and press down against
the channel's ridge.

My knees will dig into the gravel, and my legs will stretch back
toward the pond that fills twice a day
at high tide.

Water will flow through me, into all my openings and channels.

I will lie down. I will lie down.

My voice will speak through its mouth —
Its mouth will speak through my voice.

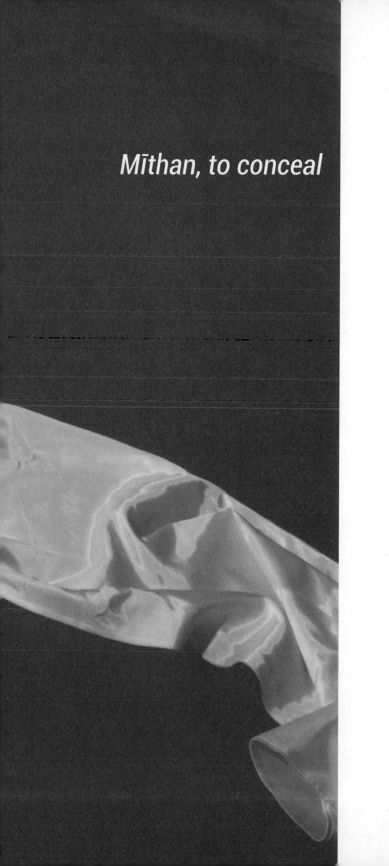

Mīthan, to conceal

A Dug Well

I have it here. In the well. She is standing by the door,
half shoulder turning. Her dressing gown half open,
a pattern, black on brown and the nipples
blown and rose burnt-brown, she
holds him soft, downy head against her arm,
she lays him down.

The rose burns brown, her skin inside the gown
a shadow, shade. Her face —

I will never have a sister now. We will be divided. Out by the well, girls
waiting for our picture. She on one side of the metal swing and I on the other.

My doll is in the middle. A secret. Our mother has a baby coming, and we do not know. We do not
know our days are numbered.

In the spring he was already in her. In the spring white bitter narcissus in the side yard. We call
them June lilies because they bloom in early June. And they are white. Their stems are hollow, and
a sticky liquid streams down when you pick one or break it.

He will be like that. A boy. A different creature, loved and wanted. A liquid animal, suckling. Who
cries. And needs her. Late, late in August. After summer. After heat.

Now drought. The wells are dry.

Now Ricky comes and tells me about the deer. Tammy and Bobby striking the doe, driving late, too
fast (he says). But stopping first to pick the white narcissus. Like Ellen and Jerome that spring when
they were young. Jerome still strong as the ox. Bent with a spade to dig up the narcissus. No one
living there, the house torn down. Holes in the ground where they dug.

The deer took off. And Ricky found it in the well. The old green well-house fallen in, and the deer
running. Circle of fixed stones. A dug well. Open.

Tempest

Low hills, and a little dog in a blue coat. His owner
a burly grey scruffled man in a pale blue jacket. The dog
on a red leash hurries after him. Clouds, rain-laden and grey
pull across these bending trees, one tall hackmatack and a maple.

Air blown across a glass bottle, wind winding up its coil of tension.
Your face. I want to touch these roiling clouds piling across in a thick band, amber
gold turning inward, rolling until my whole body falls into them, wrapped
in this envelope of cloud.

The way the muscles in your forearms twine and pull when you reach for me, the flute
of your thumb and two outer fingers. The way you look when I look into you.

Now the rain drums straight down into my taut skin.
I turn face down and wait for you.

A siren, distant. The break-shot of thunder, crack and rock. These last two days, the
weight of you, wildcat scream. Another crack. Your anger. Hammer on steel girders.

Give me the clouds. A street murder. Caravaggio diagonals and split canvas. The tower
of the old schoolhouse pitched against a reeling sky.

Storm passes over us.

We breathe, incarnate. Lucent.
Splayed.

The sky full of empty rooms

i.

The sky full of empty rooms. Wind.

My hold on earth tenuous, plants scraping the ground.
Colour washed and drained.

A white orchid, foreign, on the kitchen table, spine ridge caught in the light.
Curled vertebrae. Silence in the spaces between the chair rungs,
silence in the paint on the floor.

Mouse in the live-trap, settled in now. Wind owns the day.
Buckets upside down.

Rattle in my heart. Cough. I cannot
listen when we speak on the phone. The calls
go on forever.

Keeping it dull,
greasy as graphite. We
should stop.

ii.

Rain. Gusts of it, binding me to the house. The woodshed door opens
and flaps back. Thunder.

My heart-ropes ache.

Towels fall off the line where I hung them yesterday to air out.
Sodden. A ruination. Strands unravel, and the ping
of each string whispers ending. Poor flesh.

Hash in the pan. Potatoes and onions. Longing's
a tongue hanging out. Whiskey forever.
Trapped in the bed. No where. No else. Ask, fool,

just ask. And a bottle will clink, a toe respond, midnight
come and a strange horn resound. Pretty babies. Soft
shoes.

Listen to the sounds on the roof. Hold your heart steady.
Tick, then tock.

iii.

I hear the slip of the gravel under the boat as you push
me off. This is the boat that would carry two.

And I am one.

Bach Prelude: Reprise

What a strange and magnificent invention glass is — to be close without being stricken...
— Tomas Tranströmer, "Icelandic Hurricane"

All day the blizzard, inside the house inside the storm. The spring light lifts the wind's density, stretches it like a cheesecloth, a gauze. The spring storms enwrap and enfold, no escape, the body carried in the sound. Light reflected on ceilings, cold seeping in under the doors. Old glass, mottled and wavering, holds.

All around the house, porcupine prints, rounded, even.

From an upstairs window she sees patterns in the melting snow. The whole fabric of it, rivulets running everywhere, not random, following the lineation of the hill, the curve down to the stone wall. They must be there whenever rainwater runs — visible now as lines under the snow. The fierce blanket of the blizzard's drifts collapses under the sun. The hill falls into itself, contour lines on a map.

This is how she entered, *enters* the prelude: quiet, line by line. She takes the notes one by one, follows the pattern, each interval, with care. She dare not breathe.

The piece is too hard for her. She has not told her teacher that. She cannot.

Every piece he chooses for her is a means to stretch her, make her bold. She cringes back, wants safety. Somewhere, please God, somewhere safe.

And so, Bach's arms. Even with this degree of difficulty, the music is reliable, sure. *Sheep may safely graze* — he says so. Yes, she is far. Far inside herself. Someone should come for her and carry her home. There is no home, not now. She has crossed a line — she presses on, but slowly. Inside the music now, she begins to breathe. The notes carry her. She sings, feels the presence of harmonies she can rely on. Even the sudden transpositions in the fugue make harmonic sense. *And with His stripes — we are healed...*

The little organ loft in the chapel where she practiced is a cave. Private, a place for an animal to lie down. The fugue echoes and breaks open, at last.

She takes the notes, slow motion, follows the pattern, the whole fabric of it,
lineation of the hill, rivulets,
spring light.

Mīthan

In the barn at the old Craig house. Empty barn, no cattle for years. Still that
faint smell. And hay, the grains of it, from Timothy grass – the dust motes
in light. *Shafts*. I did not know the word then, I was fixed in light, saw the
specks like galaxies drifting down into our world, so safe, so bound – so
mutable I was and did not know that either.

Dark in daylight.

Sister star. Impossible to see. *Cast out the mote* – had I heard that yet? My small sister, fixed
on the piece of red clover she finds in the haystack, not far from the well-curb
where someone waits with a box camera – to take our picture. And I,
looking out. Facing. She is herself,

self only. And I, already other. Held face. Hair blown back.
Words, forming. *Musk, hayseed*. Attention. Watching, frown line –
point. The house – is temporary. For summer. The barn –
falling. Falling down –

The dandelion heads parachute on a breeze. Grass, mown,
turning into hay. *Swath, scythe*. Mention. Moving,
moving beyond one another. She wears a knitted beret,
perhaps pink. *The beam in your own eye*. I thought it was light, a light-
beam. I thought she saw me.

Not wanting it to end

i.

The summer, the clear early days, the unbounded sense of things continuing, the heat, the flies even, the fog, hot thick nights, the unending days. And then two days of clarity, the sun opening into a clear sky the shadows crisp, clean. There had not been shadows. The wind.

Stop it, stop. August first, second, a shift. She went (I went) – to town, twice, squandered the clear days, could not bear the intensity, did not go down to the shore, sat on the chesterfield, pulled into herself (myself). No.

Places waiting to open, to be opened to be seen. She does not (I do not) want to be seen. Does not want to look. Plain places, *the rough places plain*.

Life will end, is ending. Is always ending, but now the sense of time going on forever is impossible to sustain.

The light changes every summer, changes by increment, grass stays wet longer in the morning and the new growth is flaccid, not so easy to cut. Bees are working madly in the purple flowers, *Agastache*. Every morning large bumblebees, the thinner honeybees out back in the wild oregano. Were they there all along or have they stepped up their intensity. Fall will come, winter. She wants (I want) to hold it back.

Sound of the wind through the screen door. Not the breeze of July. Wind. August.

Rich fullness and no comfort in it now. Pearly everlasting on the side of the road, daisy family. *Anaphalis margaritacea*.

Daisy, no family. My mother loved them. Or so Dad said.

Wind in the screen, that whistling sound. Shadows under leaves, between doorways, across grass. The mornings, cold. Sun in the afternoons.

Age. I want to kill something.

Unrelenting wind.

ii.

I go mad in August. Fall out of myself. Feel the hand on my neck. I need to go lie down on the ground somewhere. Accept. Let it hold me.

As if I had a will, could do anything about what is, what comes, what will come.

The level of grass. Of grasshopper. Ant. The lily opening. Stamens red, bold, the next day covered in yellow ochre. Thick, abundant. A thing waiting to be found, fertilized.

I cannot wait like that. I can.

The fetch of the wind

Fetch: The distance wind travels over water before meeting an obstacle, like a shoreline or reef, and how it builds up a wave on the sea. A long fetch of the wind will produce larger and larger waves.

My mother travels over the fetch of the wind, eddies and curls towards me.
On this day of the storm I feel her coming in curves and circles, see her shoulders
wet – from swimming. I hear her voice. She is moulding me, moving a message
into me that I can neither understand nor comprehend. My muscles
feel her and I know she is somewhere near.

I feel my feet kicking against her belly, or is it her feet
against mine – I want to slide out and away.
But she holds me.

Listen. You have to tell this story of your eye. Your eyes.
You will not go blind. Listen, she says, One eye sees, and one
does not. What do you see, now, in the place you
have no sight –

And we are at the bright green, glassy sea. A shape in the breakers dives
and dives again. Hears me singing, high up and steady. Curls and goes under.

My mother, swimming. Free and so long dead.
Arms breaking the surface – bend, up, over,
breathe – sure in the Australian crawl. Bend,
up, over – dives.

And we are in the green and glassy sea.

It is in me forever

                        the sound of oar-locks,
(row-locks, we called them). Coming with a rhythm of pulling
and the *slush* of river-water filling in the spaces beside
the oars, the holes the water makes against the pull.

Only he might remember the look of things: water, row-boat,
salt-tide, green of spruce and transparency of a day in high summer.
Cirrus cloud, rock on water, curve and trace, path lined-up – everything
in place: blood, blessing, sin, bare arms.

Force of the father returns to me. Force of memory –
to memorize – the shore, the lines, geometry of things, rock's
size, position of ledge, sure recognition. Thing against
thing, height, shape, tree's density, power of pull.

How you line up objects with the stern of the boat
and keep a straight course rowing. Black-green of spruce, immovable,
the osprey's look-out. Ancient pulse, inside me,
laid out bare on the ground.

Vindauga

Aorta of apple, great split heart —

Brachia of the tree, curves carrying the life, the long
branches dragged down by new apples. Laden, lead,
laide. Strange beauty of pregnancy, body pulled
toward earth, barely standing by the end.

Deliver me of apples, the rich days of August — crickets'
maddening rasp insistent in the grass, seals howling
on the ledges in the river at low tide — moon
pulling the belly until the waters break.

Wind hole, breach of my roof. Wind eye
that pierces the dome of my dwelling.

Vindr wind,
auga eye.

I cannot even say come to me. Come wind,
come eye. Restless, see me.

Let me see.

The Stanzas. Rooms.

*It is always so early in here, it is before the crossroads, before the
irrevocable choices. I am grateful for this life! And yet I miss the
alternatives. All sketches wish to be real.*
— Tomas Tranströmer, "The Blue House"

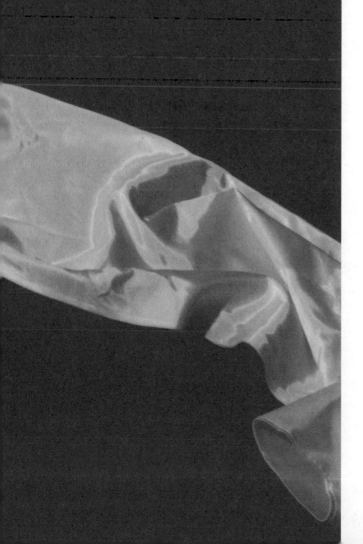

You want to say the word chemise

The computer zoom moves in on the spruce, resolution
perfect. I always said your pictures were Glenn Gould
playing Bach. All the notes clear, no background, no
foreground. Everything resolved, moving toward absolution.

The two white carousel horses, the focus, yes, but the tree equally clear. The fence clear, the clutter
of chair and wire and post and unlovely accumulation – clear. The line of undershirts and the two
white nightgowns blurred not because they are out of focus but because a breeze is blowing and
the camera has registered the movement. Everything is there.

That is why I fell in love with you. The music. The recorded detail. The absolute resolution in the
instant. I want to say *chemise*, match the flutter, drawn out, to the shirts on the line, the agitation
in my heart.

Even today I would drive straight to your door, wait for you to unlock the heavy bolts, fall inside.
Leave again.

A motor far out on the water extends the horizon of the summer night.
Both joy and sorrow swell in the magnifying glass of the dew. We do not
actually know it, but we sense it: our life has a sister vessel which plies
an entirely different route. While the sun burns behind the islands.
— Tomas Tranströmer, "The Blue House"

for George

So now it is my turn, to lay it down on paper — for you.

March — April 2017

It could have been that morning or the next afternoon they
walked up to the little graveyard, or parked the Volkswagen
Rabbit on the side of the road, and looked together at the
gravestones, aunt and grandmother, Everett, Annie, Mary
and Abie, Jennie under the glass lid that the horse broke, the cedars
nearby, and he said, 'The Russians kneel down in the snow,' flakes
were falling, November, bare. 'The Rowanberries.' She knew
them as Mountain Ash.
                          I remember his thumbs, how his hands
looked, flat on the table, fingers swollen because of the chemicals
in the developer fluid from the photographs. His hair
long then and curls, snow catching and the quiet all around, not
only the outside quiet, but the stillness around us, each instant
etching itself though it seemed just natural, sequential, like
the night before when we had made love.

The opening, the newness, as if it were now, not the
thing we say past, and impossible, the heart softening
to follow any lead, in the rabbit tracks, squirrel marks, it was

so cold that night, no heat anywhere only the wood stove,
and climbing the stairs, these stairs, staring at the old wallpaper,

a lurch in the inevitability and just so close, heart to heart.
The opening now in a flood, the other half listening – to
Tranströmer's cadence, as the ship plies its way

on that trajectory, not ours, *While the sun burns behind the
islands*, must this be, this must be, still as breath, the lamp
hot against the cold glass, feast unwrapped on the table, a knock,
the fight, intrusion, your arm along the table's edge, sleeve,

wool tweed of your jacket, protection, steady as night. Had
I never had that before? Champion, immovable, errant knight –

In an afternoon, at your house — You had just come back from flying,
somewhere, Toronto. *He who has been alone so long* — something you wrote
(how did you write to me?) or said — *enters into the light, at last.* I can still

see your handwriting — You did, you brought me Joy, Patou. *Alone so long,*
how did I not hear that? And when I asked (so many years later) 'Bring me
perfume,' what was I looking for? How did I know you wouldn't trust me

not to leave you? Sitting at the blue painted kitchen table, drinking Scotch
and as usual I was crying. (About to.) You always affected me like that, never
missing anything.
                    That other afternoon, the first one. Beethoven, 4th
piano concerto, Silverman, the pianist — you, walking down the hall towards
the bedroom, sound rippling everywhere, the luxury of it, thinking we were home
forever. Intimacy, no — surety, of those opening chords — Intimacy

in the answer, response. Did you know that when you chose the disc?
Strength, and power, and passion of you — Would It make any difference,
now — if you were able to hear me? *Yes. Yes, more than enough* —
and at so many levels. Perfect meeting. I was so afraid.

49

Not of you. Of the capturing. And the loss – the other
trajectories, sister ship, the clear-drawn lines of the
other path. *Clang!* Four times the funeral chord at *Zhivago's*
opening, the moment I happened to enter the theatre, then
the nailing, clods of earth. Eros and Thanatos. More like gates,
closing, and the boy's face – *Clang, clang, clang.*

When you married
Susan, 'Iron-clad vows...,' I didn't go. Trees – are silver this morning,
coated in ice. Late, wild spring, stupid, flooded heart. The long
opening scene, sun on the Urals, a procession in the landscape,

then the boy, the mother, wax, you were younger, and yours
came back. Severed. When you took, made, the first photograph,

you said, 'Now you're immortal,' it was a love pledge (we laughed,
and shuddered). All love is like that before it is tamed. Everything
spilled out of me, turned to you, uncensored, unafraid.

Now, on YouTube, the camera catches the violist's intense
focus on the pianist, second movement, opening, violist

lifts the instrument into his chest. You came and stood, silent
by the bed in a purple cape, long to the ground. Moonlight,

streetlight, I had cried myself to sleep like a child, friends
become enemies, the fight with the man I was pledged to, you

wanted to do something to help me – Let me go back, there was terror,
the smashed pea-green Beetle, mine, in your driveway, the huntsman

sent to find Snow White, *her heart and her liver* in a bowl, the stand-in
car, a baseball bat, neighbours calling police. And we stayed on

in the Gulag, you called it, after the ultimatum in the kitchen,
the six pictures we made in the freezing cold, washed my face

in the bathroom sink, I could drink cognac then, soot smudge
on my forearm, and your intense, focused, dear, endangered face.

Heat from the photo lamps, the great Sinar, Swiss-made
view camera, its presence in the kitchen. We fused in that
adrenaline from the confrontation, a turning toward art,

no questions. I saw you, let you. Felt the hand on the tiller.
'Sit. No, stay there.' First chair (there were three). You must
have outlined the positions, given me titles: First one, 'What

the photographer saw.' I was used, already, to entering
the lens. No one can 'take' an image – the subject, model,
has to give it. (He knew how to wait.) One quick move,

and you're out of the frame. When we made love that night
we were already changed. I had chosen to stay. Free, against you –
Or, if we didn't it was from the aftermath, the naming: The

Huntsman (let's call him that), who'd tracked me down, his rage.
I felt free – against you, your back, arms, your legs. Head like a ram's.
Year of the Sheep, both of us. Who made coffee? a fire? whose feet
hit the cold floor first? All I remember is warmth, your steady flame –

Enraptured. Christmas morning at your house, two boiled eggs in their shells,
jam and croissants, Venus, nude at breakfast. 'Little Scarlet Tiptee Strawberry
Preserve' (you can read the label in the precision of the view camera's focus),

coffee in the gold-rimmed cups. To remember like that. What does this do,
now. For what: a reprieve? Some unasked for gift. Grief unravelled, release
from the Gulag, prisoners stumbling out into the light? *Kneel down*. In the snow.

Forgive me. Only the passions whelm like this, make ikons. Do not ask. *Fidelio:*
A ladder against a window in a stage wall. My suitcases still in your front hallway,
orange, zipped, bought for touring. Police car circling the crescent. Were we? Prisoners,

joined, and now come to be released? Step into the story. I wore my wedding dress
that Christmas morning, hair a facsimile of my bride's day French braids. Because

you asked. Or was that my idea. Buttons all the way down – the train, satin, crossed tails
spreading against the floor, 'Fallen Bird,' the title. Unrepentant (your word) Romantics.

Not then. Now. Then – we were looking for the next way in, next picture. *Nest*.

The two Polish chairs. Pale blue velvet, gone now — another robin's nest.
Face to face, side by side. And that contraption you made to start a fire
in the fireplace. Red, and turquoise, that one colour photograph from Toba Tucker
your fellow artist, Navajo. Turquoise for luck, the place just above the heart.

You would walk me around the house, show me the difference between this print,
that one. George Tice, Eddie Weston. Hold yours beside theirs until they met the standard.
This is the turning point. Where can we lay down our heads? *Yet once a little while
and I will shake — the heavens, the earth* — Handel, *Messiah*. Can you have patience?

We were so very young. Everything was beauty, such a strange word, so
out-of-fashion. When I ordered white roses (a dozen) for the opening of your
show, in Boston. When we stayed at the Copley Plaza. Yes. Children. Grown up.
When we got sick (violently) from the after-party's Hungarian food, the Bull's Blood —

When you needed to come home early, cutting our time for August Sander's (heart-tearing)
portrait of the German people, I did not understand 'two-ness' — that *Refiner's fire*.

I can still see you, us. Side by side at Logan Airport. Silent. *Antlitz der Zeit*.
We must have gone to the museum that morning, rushed for the earlier flight,
I had no experience of 'marriage,' the other's needs, Sander's pictures, your work:

portrait of the blind girl and the boy standing next to a brick wall. She holds her hand
flat out on the air describing something only he can see. The boy might be deaf.
I look again: they are both blind, blind children together, and she protects him, holds
his hand close in to her side – He is wearing a padded apron, stands with both feet, in
leather boots, close together. For whom does she make the gesture?

I was made of appetite, stamina, hours in the museum, the friend I'd intended us
to meet. In our luggage, the transparent black blouse I would wear, lipstick circles
drawn around my nipples. We must have shopped before your show. We both signed
the pictures, my signature, yours. Black ink. (No lover had ever bought me clothes.) All

these years later I ask you the question. The Nazis broke Sander's glass plates. Some
he buried in the garden. Both Jews at risk and SS officers leaving for the front came to his
studio before departure. 'How tall is your brother?' Sander asks the girl. She stands,
strong, both feet planted, face toward the lens. *Blindgeborene Kinder*.

Every Sunday morning we would set off: Boxes with the photo lights. The Sinar. My make-up, clothes. Climb stairs. *The sea and the dry land...* precious little of each. Let's go back. Once upon a time, a performance artist, barely formed, made a piece

(as we said then) at a certain art gallery in Halifax, a performance piece, *Miss X*, in a borrowed fox-fur coat, silver, over a gold-thread, black, tailored coat-dress, hair a wild curled mass, plastic (false) eye-lashes, composite of several divas. Looking

back, a gay man in drag. *Marlene*. Red mouth. Students in the elevator whispering, *She's from Montreal...* And on the walls of that gallery (just happened) the work of one (as yet) unknown photographer, an early show, pure, classic eight-by-ten contact prints,

enough to stop her in her tracks. And when he stepped by accident into her make-shift dressing room – him in his. They would likely agree on the beginning, how

she pulled off her t-shirt the way you do, in a dressing room, and changed, right there into day clothes, two friends (another part of the story) nearby, one

of whom, until now, had been the sole artist who drew her, sometimes in water, *as if* she were in water, and where The Huntsman was, that day – ? Somewhere pounding nails into wood. Building, dreaming. On land.

Something about the dark. Night out the windows, black. Unadorned and unprotected, no curtain to draw around, across. And that was how he looked at her. Not through. Into. Without judgement. 'What do you love,' he'd asked, 'the way things look or the way

things are?' She chose 'looked.' His was 'are.' On that day, though, he followed her to the gallery parking lot. They were in mid-conversation. *Pictures with you.* This happened a lot. (Photographers...) A suitcase going into the little pea-green VW. *I think*

I am leaving town soon. Already decided. The Huntsman had already been hunting. Although she did not know, she knew. Hunting for her. Making shots with his camera: 35mm. By now they had an apartment in town. In the city – though what she remembers is a window

in the bedroom of the house on the side-road, Pentz, not far from the ferry at LaHave. Desdemona's window. How many years. She still drives by there. Recognizes the house. The school up the road where the boy went, would go. If they pulled it together. Two boys.

Almost home. It was the older one, fifteen, who answered the phone that Wednesday night: 'Dad's not here.' *In on it.* They drove the Rabbit back from her parents' place. Or she did,

by herself. Gone up there to make the call. 'Dad' spent Wednesdays with his daughter. Supposed to. *Bye baby bunting –*

What were they doing. Alone in that old house. She'd left him there, said nothing, she hardly knew him yet. There is only so much time. When you're in it — it seems like forever. *Daddy's gone a-hunting.* And now he'd put his foot in the snare for her and save her neck. His

face began to blotch with the redness of strife, his worry. Then she made a fire in the stove, they unwrapped their feast, and the gods of beauty and entrapment, and liberation, and silence, and pure uncontaminated joy *came upon them* — And The Beast, her Huntsman,

burst through the front door. His truck. Across the road. By the barn. His boots, so loud. His sweaters and jackets in the trunk in the front hall. Already a new world in the kitchen.

They'd been poor, and now packets of ham and sliced cheese, olives in bowls, fresh bread. Wine. Alsatian, perfect for seafood. Aphrodite. The *whore* of Venice, *The Virgin of the Rocks.* This Beast had spent everything. For her. And now she'd spent everything. For this Stranger. Had she been alone —

But she was not. His sleeve, his arm at an angle on the pine wooden table. His gaze. And not one word. As The Huntsman exploded, hauled up a chair between them, a little away, the triangle, angle of the triangle in place. John the Baptist come to proclaim from the desert —

Honey and locusts. A man in pain. They might have gone undetected for a very long time, until she'd said, 'If you want to see me as I really am, we'll have to go to the house. At Sable.' And she made the plans like a pro, said she'd meet the plumber, mid-week, get the work started, not afraid to stay there alone. And then she packed. Everything. All her clothes, diaphragm, shampoo, the photographer's shirt she'd said was Sarah O's. The

whirlwind. She had not faced her truth. The way he cut his eggs-on-toast. Silent. Parallel lines across, and then at right angles, again. The way he'd thrown her (she was willing) on the kitchen floor at Pentz every night after dinner. The photo she called 'Desdemona,' dead on the bed, the blue satin dressing-gown with magenta pink trim. The night he'd put his foot on her neck. And

meant it. She was betrothed. Her house, dowry. Her father addressed this man directly now, by-passed her. Just as he brought her wood, her other grandmother's chairs – for the house down the road – his allegiance changed. This builder's

sense of rightness, entitlement, his will to stop her flight. All summer long. Birds, dead birds against the windscreen of the VW Beetle, pea-green. Hers. And now it's in the driveway at Tangmere and she –

In this last hour – has been called 'whore,' 'strumpet,' 'faithless,' 'cunning,' one who'd give up everything. *For a fuck* – or so he thinks. Stillness is her weapon. Has always been her weapon. Silent. Immobile. In the trap. The situation is reversed.

How she knows she does not know. There is a plot. And her Emilia's faithless – wants her caught. Knots design a path – of thorns. Apples redden, dark unwinds the night. She stands upon a bridge. Another story. It's to herself she's faithful. Something shines inside

her face. This one who stands beside her. Sees her. Artist, singular, he sees her, not an aspect of himself or even of his longing. The thing that no one wants her to become.

She swims into her firmament. Meets him. In the frame. And now the bridge: *Ah! non credea mirarti, I did not believe*... Read this – as the bride who crosses to herself. Read

this – as the return. Both then – and now. His gift – to protect her. Of course, though not of necessity – she will fly away. But we are not there yet. She stands

on the bridge. On the tightrope across the chasm. And he does not waver. Nor does she. In the kitchen, before the pictures. In the moment – she faces her attacker, holds her ground. And screams. A voice. She has a voice.

The vulnerability that doesn't show. The ways we don't see one another.
The presence of now, immediacy, a day in April, letter in the mailbox. *You
say I used you*. How did I use you? How did the ones who married you

not? You can see how untutored I am, how unskilled in the ways of courting
love. To have these questions still. How a large and clever feline would lick
a paw and slowly shut her eyes. How a wife will turn, and smile, because
she's made her vows. The wild one never can come home. *Well then? Ebben?*

I'll go far away. Ne andrò lontana... That aria in the centre of a film. Opera! In hours —
what a lifetime takes to live. *Diva*. And so not so. A hundred, thousand hours. That

letter in a black envelope, the one that reached me in Vancouver. Why do I think
of sheep in a field. 'He walked into the water. And then he walked out.' Pneumonia,

and loneliness, like Keats. Stupid, stupid heart. I know — the hours and days
and lives have passed. Mine have. A curse to unravel, ravelling still. Lungs,
lumen, light. Grief. And all that came after. *La Wally*. Falling into the avalanche.

Should I tell you now? Go on with the story until I find my way?
There's no changing how a thing has been for thirty years. No
spilling – I will not say 'unshed tears.' We haven't had Verykino,

Life is not a walk across a field. It was a walk that day we visited
my family's graveyard. You have no idea how I've imagined 'husband,'
a word I never say. It's sacred only to the one who cannot say it. You kept

my wedding dress. The boy I married's lived a life with someone tangible
and real. What kind of estrangement should I have to bear before this story's
out? Acceleration. The speed at which we travelled. Parted stars. I don't remember

how that happened. I know it did. You think the one who leaves holds all the power.
She does not. Not so. But light has seeped beneath the prison door. Light has slipped
between the louvered slats and stabbed the corners of the rooms. We'll stop, and carry

one another, but first I'll have to cross. It isn't simple, is it – to open what's been sealed
and settled, finished, burnished. You want me scraped down, no patina. I want you – now.

Or have we lived it. Been there. Verykino. The ice-palace where I live
in winter. Shall I tell you now, or wait until we meet, risk being tongue-tied,
or too articulate to speak — feeling. Wrapped in my own rabbit skin. Intelligence,

the ability to see and stay blind. Have you heard a rabbit's heart beat when the snare
comes round the neck, fir bough bent just right, passageway on the indented, indentured
path? And then it stops. I can see this thing a hundred different ways. I want to see

what you see. Stop. Know. What must be. *Muss es sein? Es muss sein!* 'The difficult
decision.' There isn't any decision now. Feeling — and a willingness to feel. *How*

did I use you: Does the Muse use the Artist. Artist use the Muse? It's more
than that. I want to take off my clothes and lie down with you, naked
and armed to the teeth. When the narratives stop, will the armour fall?

Vulnerable, that's where we started. It's now — the vulnerability that doesn't,
didn't, show. Rabbit runs zig-zag to out-run, baffle The Wolf. Bobcat, the elusive

one we never see. I had a coat like that, wide, thick-woven tweed, cut all the stainless-
steel snare-wires when I followed the hunter's tracks. No metaphor. I cut them,
brought them back in the pockets of that coat. *Wrapped his baby bunting in.*

It's not the heart. It's the cry. The rabbit's voice. I've heard it once, that winter
after I'd moved back here. So. Now. Was that his voice? Mine? What must I do.
What must be? Listen to that late Beethoven quartet, then come back and talk

to me. What can I swear – that feeling matters, matters now? Dear, beloved
once-upon-a-time, dear beloved – now. Dear reader – if you have not thrown
the book, or turned the page. The parts that I've erased! The coat I bought
to mitigate love's pain. The woman I loved and ran from, no coming back

from that. Elegant, expensive tweed, with pockets. A camouflage – black
and brown and white and yellow-beige. Worn in a field – to baffle a cat so smart
I saw it only once, how it turned, defiant, when I came upon its kill, the deer haunch.

What's pursuing me – Your words, your letter's thrown me off: *You used me!* (His
story will persist. She does not own it all.) 'A voice. She has a voice!' Can we stand
beside, or alternate? Dissonance – and harmony. Your lovers, mine. Atonement. Let
me tell the story, let down Rapunzel's hair. It isn't pretty. Someone loses an eye.

The tension's gone. The love flows out of me, flows toward and unabated. I'd kneel
down and break the alabaster box. Let all the perfumed ointment out. Photographer.
The man inside the lens. The one who sees. Who stands outside, gives his whole self –

Lento assai, cantante e tranquillo, very slow, like a singer. The light freezes
a line around her mouth — he makes the shot. But wait. Let's do this tonight. If,
perchance there is no tomorrow — and 'this' is Beethoven's Quartet # 16, Opus 135.

I'm giving you this link so you can find the music in case it's something you
don't already happen to know. (The photographer knows, knows it all
from the first mention.) As if this were a night we'd spend together. As if

you could imagine how many — among the hundreds of references a lifetime offers,
and collects — there are in common. *To us.* I want to draw the curtain back. I want
to close it shut. Either way we have to listen to this music, the slow movement

in particular. The tenderness. *Patience.* There will be time. Foolishness,
I want to say. But this is not. Just listen. And then we will go on. Years earlier

in the spirit of this quartet, Beethoven wrote a letter, the Heiligenstadt Testament:
I must live like an exile — if I approach near to people a hot terror seizes upon me...

As much a letter as a last will and a confession, sealed. To himself.
*What a humiliation when one stood beside me and heard a flute in the distance
and* I heard nothing. *To my art I owe the fact that I did not end my life...*

We've come so far. The light, today, is hard – spring, April light, bare lilacs fall
in shadows on the hard clay road. A lamp post. And lilac trunks are rippled,
patterns, curved. Her mouth. He makes the shot. In the second chair – this one's

the shock – he says, 'Sit there,' and indicates The Huntsman's seat: 'What
the woman saw.' To see – what he said I was. Become The Beast that came to take me,
make me what he needed me to be. *His whore.* And all the vomit, power, terror

of The Wolf possesses me. The seer guides, but lets me stand alone. 'You can point.
And you can shoot – and you can frame.' You cannot make reality. You stare it –
in its face. The bond we make that night is something I, perhaps, have not yet

understood. His stillness. Stance. There cannot be – many – moments of actual love. Perhaps
that's why, in opera – they come with death. But this is life he offers me. I step

into the frame. And – in the third chair: 'What the man (The Huntsman) saw,' there –
the scream, the voice, the filling of a soul into herself – recounted. And she will burn his

presence from the house. But now, to stand, to feel, to know – to hold – her place. They
let the fires of transmutation play upon them. So new, so young – to walk into the flame
that making art demands. They cannot know they'll lose it all. Or if they'll find it –

The boards are bare. *I am grateful for this life! And yet I miss the alternatives.* Yesterday, yes, April, looking into the dining room, the blazing four o'clock light, white, lined Ikea curtain looped across the window at the back. The French doors you wouldn't

recognize. Not to count the years. *All sketches wish to be real.* And they are, until it stops. This stops. And you're not here. Presence. So palpable. We have to know. We know. What shall we gather up. The Rowanberries? Those trees will blossom white

this June, red berries will come in fall and someone say the winter will be long – and cold – if they're abundant. I am so alone. I am. I don't have you! Might not be able to stand you, or you me. This is my habitat and oh, you have yours. Necessity. The place in which

one has to live. To breathe, not only function – Breathe. Flourish. Work. 'The photo bunker,' yours. A whole house – in which to write. Excessive. Mine. Blood – and flesh. Let desire come.

It comes. Let the deluge, flood – No coming to your door. No disruption. *I lie.* It's all disruption, asked for, called for, waited – and unstrung. And nothing to be done. The sister ship's

plied on – I can write to you, or put it here – for everyone. The thing you do that scares me. Coward. Yes, I am. Your – viscera. I promised, though, to pull the threads together. What's missing, what wants telling. Still. Her face. In water. In the creek. Oh – this still unwritten life.

Coda, Aubade.

On the other side is open terrain. Formerly a garden, now wilderness...
Above the overgrown garden flutters the shadow of a boomerang,
thrown again and again.
— Tomas Tranströmer, "The Blue House"

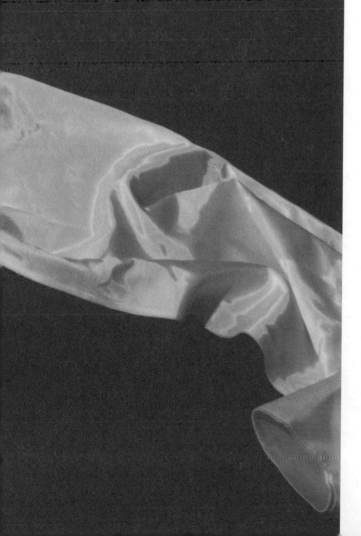

The way white lilacs start to open, slow in the cold spring rain. Late May, greenish yellow light, the heart-shaped leaves giving way to an eruption in the tight furled blossoms at the end of each stem. Lilac trees, old

beyond comprehension. When he was twelve, Warren Decker shouted for me to come when he'd sawed open a lilac branch. Mauve, he said. And it was. A round of purple at the core. I am tired. Still blossoming. Spring

always comes, light in the dark. Amethyst. The white lilacs drift like snow. Early June, the wind blows east nor' east and plants cringe in the ground. The lilacs toss and sway, white as cocaine, my heart swims. This cannot be

my life. Winter in spring. (Too late to stop the blossom.) Something will shift, wind blowing off the ice mid-river. A drowning. You will not come back. What

drives the heart — to view a life lived backwards, unspooling. Now I see your face, washed, as night slides into day. I wanted it to stop. Here. Your shoulders,

arms. A beating, pulse, to push us onward, unresisting. You said *everything is still possible.* I found your handwriting on the stairs. That letter slipped open in a midden of paper. Still. Shimmering in the morning wind. And gone.

To float, to drown...

The place of the title poem is East Sable River, Nova Scotia, a village on the east side of the Sable River, its orientation defined by the river's direction. The river flows approximately north to south; the sun rises on its east side and sets over the west. Like most rivers that flow directly into the sea, the Sable is tidal, but what distinguishes it is the distance the tide travels inland. When the ocean tide rises, it enters the peat-brown waters of the Sable and flows up for several miles against the river's current, bringing salt sea water in through the river's mouth to mix with fresh water from the inland brooks and bogs that drain down into the headwaters of the river's origin. A river has both a "head" and a "mouth," and as children we grew up hearing this language before we knew enough to question it.

The village houses are built along the road that runs beside the river that gives us our directions: upriver is "up the road" and downriver—towards the sea—is "down the road." Across the river is the west side, and further down on that side is a long stretch of beach. Our language is "tied to the land," to the river, the round of tides, the cycle: each day high tide is close to one hour later than the day before, low tide follows the same pattern, and the time between the two is about six hours. Not all of this is made explicit in the poems, but memory from childhood is embedded in this world.

The memories arrive in fragments; various pieces loom large or small, details float in and fall away. Saltmarshes border the river on either side, sandflats fill the centre following the channel, the tides come and go, and down near the river's mouth on the east side a creek runs through a large tidal estuary across an acre of saltmarsh that opens into the sea. This is our world—and this world lies under much of the rest of the book. The origins of language in childhood never go away.

p. 3
the small old house
The small house (referred to in the family, and in the poem, as "the old house") was Cape Cod style, simple, no dormers, with an extension at the back end of the house facing the road and the kitchen door on the side. The main part of the house faced the river, pointing to a time before the road when travel was by boat, and there would have been a dock or at least a slip at the river's edge. This was my paternal grandparents' house, built c. 1830 by Josiah Ridgeway, the property purchased by Everett Pierce, my grandfather who married Jennie Anderson from Louis Head, near the beach across the river. Her mother was a Ridgeway, so the house and property may have been part of an inheritance. Jennie died in childbirth in 1898 when she was twenty-five, and Everett later married Annie Crouse from Beach Meadows who raised his first three children and bore twelve more, one of whom was my father. This house is no longer standing.

p. 6
the Tom Tigney
The Tom Tigney River is a tributary of the Sable. It is a fresh-water river, not tidal like the Sable, and flows under a bridge at the highway that runs through the larger upriver community of Sable River.

p. 8
Two houses, one up the road, one down
The houses that dominate the title poem are situated a mile apart from one another. These are the grandparents' houses, and that mile constitutes the centre of the child's world.

The smaller house, whitewashed, old
The paternal grandparents' house seen in comparison to the big house of the maternal grandparents looks small and old. This house was whitewashed, rather than painted. "Whitewash" was made from a mix of lime and water with glue size added so the mixture would adhere to the wood.

Sides banked with eelgrass for winter
In winter, the houses were "banked," which means they were surrounded by a wooden structure about two feet high filled with dried eelgrass from the shore to help keep the interior warm. There was little or no other insulation and only the wood stove for heat.

Low roof, ell chamber
An "ell" is an extension to a house or outbuilding built at a right angle to the main structure, thus forming an L shape. The "ell chamber" referred to here was a tiny bedroom over the pantry off the kitchen in the ell. The little chamber was accessible off the large bedroom upstairs under the sloping roof and could be entered by climbing over a large beam.

p. 9

The other house, the one down the road

This house was built in 1905–06 for my maternal grandparents, Abram Stanley Lloyd and Mary Mitchell Swansburg Lloyd. Like many houses in Nova Scotia, this one, built by master carpenter Charles Robertson along with Abie Lloyd and men from the village, combines a mix of styles including elements of Scottish Vernacular and Victorian Eclectic. It has three stories with a full second floor and attic, as well as four bedrooms. The house has a front veranda, cross-hipped roof, clapboard and shingles, large sash windows, and decorative trim. Some aspects of the interior show the influence of the Arts and Crafts style, not typical of other houses in the village. Mary and Abie had five children, the youngest of whom was my mother. This house, where I live now, is "down the road" from the smaller house, further downriver. It sits on a hill past the mouth of the river and overlooks a pasture next to the creek that runs through a saltmarsh and flows into the sea.

p. 13

A chorus from the church, cracked voices stretching up

The East Sable River Port L'Hebert Community Church was designed by Charles Robertson and built in 1906. The entire interior, ceiling and walls, is made of tongue-and-groove pine with scalloped detail in highly varnished wood. The church features lancet windows and simulated corner buttresses. For a time when there were two congregations, Baptist and United (newly formed from the Presbyterian, Methodist, and Congregational Union churches), members met on alternate Sundays according to their preference. There was always a choir, and four-part singing.

p. 14

Bach's *Well-Tempered Clavier*

Known to musicians as WTC I and WTC II (affectionately, also, as "the forty-eight"), this work forms the foundation of nearly every keyboard musician's technique. Johann Sebastian Bach wrote two sets of twenty-four preludes and fugues, a pair in each of the keys (one in the major key, one in the minor) that make up the twelve semi-tones of the chromatic "tempered" scale of a keyboard instrument. Bach wrote the first series of twenty-four preludes and fugues in 1722, and the second set some twenty years later while he was Thomaskantor in Leipzig, where he served from 1723 to 1750.

One of the diabolical sonatas, all pattern and bravura

Beethoven's Piano Sonata in B-flat major, Number 11, Opus 22: this sonata is technically difficult and requires a bold attack.

p. 15

following the chromatic intervals of the Bach prelude

J.S. Bach, Prelude and Fugue #20 in A-minor, WTC II, the second book of the *Well-Tempered Clavier*: the prelude is based on a descending chromatic theme.

Sheep may safely graze...
This is the text of a well-known soprano aria from J.S. Bach's Cantata 208, also known as the "Hunting Cantata." The solo piece is often sung as a chorus and has been transcribed as well for solo piano and for a two-piano version. The text sometimes appears as "Flocks in pastures green abiding..."

p. 16
The introduction, spoken to the audience, is an apology for love
A paraphrase of pianist Angela Cheng's introduction to her performance of the Beethoven Opus 110 recorded for CBC Radio.

The great 110, in A-flat major
This is one of the last three Beethoven piano sonatas, Opus 109, 110, and 111, written between 1820 and 1822. (Beethoven died in 1827.) Of the 32 piano sonatas, Opus 110 is #31.

p. 17
Now all the youth of England
The quotations in this passage set in italic are from Shakespeare's *Henry V*, spoken by the Chorus. There are references to *Henry IV* Part I and Part II in this segment as well.

p. 19
he stands in the kitchen of the new house he built so long ago
My father built the new house over the cellar hole of the old house he tore down and burned. The new house has the same orientation to the river and the road as did the old one, although it is larger by far and of a different style, and the front door now faces the road. There is no "ell."

p. 28
Water from the water-brook will pour out and make its gurgling sound
Always, as a child, I wondered why my grandmother called our brook "the water-brook." Aren't all brooks water-brooks? Some time after I wrote the poem, a hand-made sign appeared at the side of the road near this brook, "The Otter Brook," and my neighbour told me about seeing otters in there when he was a child.

p. 35
Bach Prelude: Reprise
The prelude referred to in this poem's title is from Bach's Prelude and Fugue #20 in A-minor, WTC II, one of the 24 preludes and fugues of the second book. The prelude is based on a descending chromatic theme, or figure, plaintive in nature, interior, quiet. This is the same A-minor prelude that appears earlier in the long poem, "To Float, to drown...".

And with His stripes — we are healed
The fugue subject bears a strong resemblance to the opening theme of the chorus "And with His stripes we are healed" from Handel's *Messiah*. Either Bach's or Handel's theme could have derived from the other, given the dates of composition. This echo of the words from the Handel chorus offers the possibility or suggestion of healing even in the fugue's subject, the motif on which a fugue is constructed.

p. 36
Mīthan
This poem title comes from the etymology of "mutable," Middle English, from Latin *mutabilis*, from *mutare* to change; akin to Old English *mīthan* (to conceal), and Sanskrit *mināti* (he exchanges, deceives).

Cast out the mote — had I heard that yet?
From the Bible, part of the Sermon on the Mount, Matthew 7, verse 5, KJV: "...first cast out the beam out of thine own eye, and then shalt thou see clearly to cast out the mote out of thy brother's eye."

p. 41
Vindauga
The title for this poem is taken from an Old Norse word derived from *vindr* (wind) and *auga* (eye): wind eye, wind hole.

The Stanzas. Rooms.

I met George Steeves in the fall of 1981 when I made a solo performance piece at the Mount Saint Vincent University Art Gallery in Halifax. George's photographic work, a show of 8x10 contact prints was displayed in the upper gallery, and the gallery director invited him to see my performance and to meet me. Two weeks later we met at a dance studio for our first photo session, and decided to continue, first to photograph my performance persona, Miss X, and then to pursue what became an extended photographic portrait, *The Pictures of Ellen*. Within a month we were lovers and colleagues and we lived together until 1984. Our relationship continued in various ways, and although we parted as a couple, the bond between us and our connection through *The Pictures* never stopped.

In the spring of 2017 I wrote George on his birthday at the beginning of March and sent him "You want to say the word *chemise*." We began exchanging letters and email and George told me *The Pictures* were in photo boxes in the hallway at Tangmere (his residence), ready to be transported to the Montreal Museum of Fine Arts. At the end of that month I began writing

"The Stanzas," telling myself the story of our beginnings, the memory coming in fragments as it does. (*Stanza* is Italian for room.)

There are two iterations of *The Pictures of Ellen*, one in the permanent collection of the National Gallery of Canada in Ottawa (24 prints), and the other at Musée des beaux-arts de Montréal (permanent collection), comprising 98 prints.

Throughout "The Stanzas. Rooms." there are references to *Doctor Zhivago*, both the novel by Boris Pasternak and David Lean's 1965 film adaptation.

p. 47
Jennie under the glass lid that the horse broke
"Jennie" is Jennie Anderson Pierce, my grandfather Everett Pierce's first wife. Her son, St. Clair Pierce, their firstborn, made a gravesite next to the white marble stone bearing her name. He placed purple mussel shells in a pattern on sand and fine gravel over which he placed an oblong glass and wood frame, then planted cedar trees nearby.

'The Russians kneel down in the snow' ... 'The Rowanberries'
The rowan tree with its red berries is a potent symbol connecting Yuri and Lara in *Doctor Zhivago* (see especially chapter 12 in Pasternak's novel). In Sable River we call this tree Mountain Ash.

p. 50
The long opening scene, sun on the Urals
The long shot near the beginning of the 1965 film adaptation of *Doctor Zhivago*, of a funeral procession and singing, is followed by a close-up of the burial of Yuri's mother.

p. 51
second movement, opening
At the opening of the second movement of Beethoven's 4th piano concerto, the strings, in unison, alternate with the solo piano stating the theme in solid chords. This is the Beethoven piano concerto referenced in one of the earlier Stanzas, "In an afternoon, at your house."

p. 53
Venus, nude at breakfast
Venus at Breakfast, Christmas 1981 is the full title of a photograph by George Steeves from *The Pictures of Ellen*.

Fidelio: A ladder against a window in a stage wall

Beethoven's only opera, composed in 1805, is entitled *Fidelio*, named after its heroine. Florestan, in prison on false charges, is rescued by his wife Leonore who enters the prison in disguise as "Fidelio." The ladder represents their escape.

'Fallen Bird,' the title

Christmas, "Fallen Bird" Ellen's Wedding Dress, 26 December 1981 is the complete title of this photograph by George Steeves from *The Pictures of Ellen*.

p. 54
August Sander's (heart-tearing) portrait of the German people

August Sander, German photographer (1876–1964), exhibit at the Boston Museum of Fine Arts: in 1936 the Nazis confiscated Sander's first published version of the project, *Face of Our Time (Antlitz der Zeit)*, and destroyed all the printing plates. Sander photographed "types" from all walks of life, the bricklayer, the pastry chef, the accountant, the artist, the young soldier, circus people with their wagon, young farmers striding across a field.

p. 55
Antlitz der Zeit

Face of Our Time is the English translation for the title of August Sander's extended portrait of the German people, which he intended first as a collection of photographs in book form.

Blindgeborene Kinder

Children Born Blind is the English translation for the title of this photograph of August Sander's, one of several in the series of this name. Sander's compassion and willingness to include people of all kinds, even those considered undesirable, put his work at risk in the Germany of the mid-1930s. The Tate Gallery (London) website is a good source for images of Sander's photographs.

p. 56
a certain art gallery

This is a reference to the Mount Saint Vincent University Art Gallery in Halifax, Nova Scotia.

p. 58
The *whore* of Venice

One of many epithets for Desdemona in Shakespeare's *Othello*: "I cry you mercy, then. I took you for that cunning whore of Venice that married with Othello." Act IV, Scene 2 (Othello addresses Desdemona and speaks of himself in third person).

The Virgin of the Rocks
In this painting by Leonardo da Vinci, the artist depicts the Virgin seated in a grotto or stone cave. There are two versions of this painting, one at the Louvre and the other in the National Gallery in London.

p. 59
Honey and locusts
John the Baptist is purported to have eaten honey and locusts in the desert. "Locusts" has a number of possible references: he may have eaten the actual insect; he may have eaten a paste or cake made from the carob plant. The Greek word for "locust" (*akrides*) is very close to the Greek for "honey cake" (*egkrides*).

in the driveway at Tangmere
This is a reference to the photographer's residence on Tangmere Crescent, in Halifax.

p. 60
And her Emilia's faithless – wants her caught
Emilia is Desdemona's faithful maid and companion in Shakespeare's *Othello*.

Ah! non credea mirarti, I did not believe...
Ah! non credea mirarti / Sì presto estinto, o fiore (I did not believe you would fade so soon, oh flower) Amina's final aria from Vincenzo Bellini's opera *La Sonnambula* (The sleepwalker): in her sleep, the heroine, Amina, steps onto a bridge over a chasm. She has spent the night, fallen asleep in the presence of a stranger, and the situation looks as if she has been unfaithful to her betrothed, Elvino. In the aria, she recounts the story of Elvino's rejection and the villagers understand that the fact of her sleepwalking explains the truth of her innocence. They dare not wake her while she is on the bridge.

p. 61
Diva
Diva is a French thriller directed by Jean-Jacques Beineix, in which the heroine sings the aria from *La Wally*, an opera composed by Alfredo Catalani that was first performed at La Scala in 1892. The opera's heroine, Wally, follows her lover into the avalanche that roars down and kills him just as they are reunited.

p. 62
Verykino
In *Doctor Zhivago*, Verykino is the remote family estate in the Urals where Yuri and Tonya move with their son Sasha when they flee Moscow. In nearby Yuriatin, Yuri finds Lara Antipova, whom he had

met in a field hospital during the war. Some years later, Yuri and Lara and her daughter Katya stay together at Verykino in winter, and Yuri begins the "Lara Poems."

Life is not a walk across a field
From a Russian proverb, the last line in Boris Pasternak's poem, "Hamlet": "I am alone; all around me drowns in falsehood: / Life is not a walk across a field." This line has been variously translated, e.g., "To live your life is not as simple as to cross a field" and "Life is not a stroll across a field." This poem, the first of the *Zhivago* poems (also known as the "Lara Poems"), though not published in the Soviet Union, was known to thousands. At Pasternak's burial, those who were present recited the banned poem by heart.

p. 63
'The difficult decision'
Beethoven wrote *Der Schwer Gefasste Entschluss* (The difficult decision, or The difficult resolution) as a title over the final movement of the work, and wrote *Muss es sein? Es muss sein. Es muss sein.* directly over the opening bars of this 4th movement of his string quartet, Opus 135, the final quartet. This quartet appears a number of times in "The Stanzas."

p. 65
Lento assai, cantante e tranquillo, very slow, like a singer
Tempo marking for the second movement of Beethoven's string quartet #16 in D-flat major, Opus 135, the *Muss es sein* quartet.

I must live like an exile...
This passage is an excerpt from Beethoven's Heiligenstadt Testament, written in October 1802 but not opened until after his death in 1827. In the spring of 1802, Beethoven went to Heiligenstadt in the countryside near Vienna for a period of rest, and in October wrote this document in the form of a letter that expressed his awareness and distress at his increasing deafness.

p. 67
I am grateful for this life! And yet I miss the alternatives
All sketches wish to be real
These quotations, which have guided "The Stanzas" from their inception, are from Tomas Tranströmer's poem, "The Blue House."

ACKNOWLEDGEMENTS

I am grateful for early readers of the title poem, "To float, to drown...": Don McKay and Barry Dempster at Banff, Jan Zwicky, Stephanie Bolster, Daphne Marlatt, and Harry Thurston. I was fortunate to work on this manuscript at several of the Writing Studios at the Banff Centre and at the Poetry Colloquia at Sage Hill. My work has benefitted from discussions and seminars with my colleagues there and with my writing group in Nova Scotia: Jan Barkhouse, Cynthia French, Veryan Haysom, Carol Laing, and Basma Kavanagh. Cynthia French and Basma Kavanagh were early readers of "The Stanzas" in the spring of 2017, along with Babo Kamel and Lesley Valdes during "The Grind." Basma stood with me at the blank page when the stanzas began to arrive; Jane Alexander read the first proofs at my kitchen table. George Steeves supported the work from its beginnings and provided the cover photograph, *Christmas, "Fallen Bird" Ellen's Wedding Dress*.

I wish to thank my poetry editor at University of Alberta Press, Peter Midgley, for his insight and understanding; my production editor, Mary Lou Roy; the marketing team, Cathie Crooks and Monika Igali; and the design team, Alan Brownoff and Denise Ahlefeldt. I have benefitted from their combined expertise and attention to detail. A special word to Cathie and Mary Lou for taking me through the final stages of production, and to Denise for her inspired design.

The sources of my support and sustenance, both spiritual and material, are many: Kate Krug, Nancy and Ron Roth, Timothy Gillespie, Les and Cynthia French, Jan Barkhouse and Greg Howard, Donna Smyth and Gillian Thomas, Basma Kavanagh and Keith Williams, Afra Kavanagh, Laine Gifford, Mary Swann, Don Hannah and Doug Guildford, Linda and Sandy Moore, Gail Daniels, Marilyn O'Neil.

Special thanks to the Shelburne County Arts Council and Susan Hoover for the Canada Council for the Arts' funded Writer-in-Residence position they secured for me, and for their ongoing support for that work since 2013.

I wish to acknowledge and thank the Canada Council for the Arts and Arts Nova Scotia for sustaining grants that provided me time in which to produce the work in its early stages. I am grateful also to the Banff Centre and to Sage Hill Writing for scholarships and bursaries that made it possible for me to be in residence for extended periods of time.

I am indebted to the following works for background, research, and inspiration: *The Zhivago Affair: The Kremlin, the CIA, and the Battle Over a Forbidden Book* by Peter Finn and Petra Couvée (Penguin Random House, 2015); *Doctor Zhivago* by Boris Pasternak, translated by Manya Harari and Max Hayward (Knopf/Everyman, 1991); and *The Great Enigma: New Collected Poems* by Tomas Tranströmer, translated by Robin Fulton (New Directions, 2006).

All quotations from Tomas Tranströmer are from *The Blue House*, a collection of prose poems translated from the Swedish by Göran Malmqvist (Thunder City Press, 1987).

* * *

A number of poems in this volume have appeared, some in slightly different versions, in the following publications. I thank the editors and publishers of each.

"To float, to drown, to close up, to open – a throat" (excerpt):
Arc Poetry Magazine #59, 2008 (Arc Poem of the Year, Honorable Mention).
The Best Canadian Poetry in English, 2008. Tightrope Books, 2008.

"Full Moon" (excerpt):
Contemporary Verse 2 (CV2), The Green Issue, Fall 2009.

"The Creek" (excerpt):
The Goose: A Journal of Arts, Environment, and Culture in Canada, Issue 11, Summer 2012.

"Medway River, Carousel"(in an earlier version):
Arc Poetry Magazine #71, 2013. (Arc Poem of the Year, People's Choice).

"The fetch of the wind":
Literary Review of Canada (LRC), March 2016.

"Bitter, salt, vital, quick" (excerpt from "To float, to drown..."):
Sustenance: Writers from BC and Beyond on the Subject of Food. Anvil Press, 2017.

"The way white lilacs" (from "The Stanzas. Rooms."):
Aubade: Poetry and Prose from Nova Scotia Writers. Boularderie Island Press, 2018.

"Vindauga":
Literary Review of Canada (LRC), March 2019.

Other Titles from University of Alberta Press

Believing is not the same as Being Saved

LISA MARTIN

Lyric poems that tenderly meditate on life and death, joy and sorrow, faith and doubt.

Robert Kroetsch Series

Little Wildheart

MICHELINE MAYLOR

Quirky, startling, earthy poems reflect the moods of existence.

Robert Kroetsch Series

There Are Not Enough Sad Songs

MARITA DACHSEL

Delicate, authentic poems that oscillate between grief and joy as they explore parenthood and loss.

Robert Kroetsch Series

More information at **uap.ualberta.ca**